Contents

How to Use This Book

The goal of *Vocabulary Development* is to help learners achieve success in language arts at a fourth-grade level. The age-appropriate activities featured in this book are based on curricula used nationwide and standards set by the International Reading Association (IRA) for developing phonemic awareness, spelling skills, and word recognition. As learners develop these skills, they strengthen their abilities in writing and reading comprehension. Kid-friendly subject matter engages learners while preparing them for achievement in language arts.

Vocabulary Development features six sections, each highlighting a different area of the fourth-grade curriculum: Vowel Sounds, Prefixes and Suffixes, Synonyms and Antonyms, Word Classification and Analogies, Homophones and Syllables, and Spelling Sounds. Each section focuses on developing specific vocabulary skills and presents four activities with easy-to-follow directions as well as skill definitions and examples.

Vowel Sounds

The first section of this book involves long and short vowel sounds. As learners practice identifying different language sounds, they develop a sense of how the sounds make up words. Recognizing sound patterns enables learners to build their word recognition skills.

Prefixes and Suffixes

The second section of this book focuses on learners' understanding of prefixes and suffixes. Learners complete activities in which they combine these words parts with root words as well as activities in which they separate root words from the word parts. In doing so, learners develop an understanding of meaning patterns and become better readers.

Synonyms and Antonyms

The third section of this book concentrates on synonyms and antonyms. Learners complete activities that expand their vocabularies by introducing words with similar and opposite meanings. The activities help learners use language effectively in their own writing by teaching them to vary their word choice.

© Rosen School Supply•Brain Builders Vocabulary Development•4•RSS-8563-6

Word Classification and Analogies

The fourth section of this book deals with developing learners' abilities to classify words and complete analogies. The activities challenge learners to recognize relationships among words, reinforcing important word-definition skills.

Homophones and Syllables

The fifth section of this book involves homophones and syllables. In completing homophone activities, learners are challenged to identify a word's definition based on how the word is spelled, not how it sounds. Learners also practice separating a word by its syllables, developing their abilities to decode words.

Spelling Sounds

In the final section of this book, learners work with various grade-appropriate spelling sounds. Activities involving the *k*, *s*, and *f* sounds help learners distinguish between the sounds they hear and the actual spelling of words. Through the identification of spelling sounds, learners improve their spelling, reading comprehension, and writing skills.

Skills Correlation Guide

	Short Vowels	Long Vowels	Word Parts	Synonyms	Antonyms	Categorization	Analogies	Homophones	Syllables	Letter Sounds
Vowel Sounds (pp. 11-15)	✓	✓								
Prefixes and Suffixes (pp. 17-21)			✓							
Synonyms and Antonyms (pp. 23-27)				✓	✓					
Word Classification and Analogies (pp. 29-33)						✓				
Homophones and Syllables (pp. 35-39)							✓	✓		
Spelling Sounds (pp. 41-45)									✓	✓

The activities featured in this book are level R according to guidelines set by Fountas and Pinnell.

© Rosen School Supply•Brain Builders Vocabulary Development•4•RSS-8563-6

Name _____

Short Vowels

 Directions: Circle the word or words in each group that have the same short vowel sound as the bold word.

1. **belt**   smell   beg   least   snail

2. **lash**   face   grasp   lace   tame

3. **rest**   toast   fetch   kneel   bench

4. **drip**   fist   drop   walk   thick

5. **plug**   play   stuck   big   shrug

6. **block**   blue   doll   clock   foot

7. **grab**   blast   grow   raft   cave

8. **skunk**   soup   duck   bun   bank

4

© Rosen School Supply•Brain Builders Vocabulary Development•4•RSS-8563-6

Name _____

Prefixes

 Directions: Circle the word in each sentence that begins with a prefix. On the lines, write the prefix and the root word.

1. A bicycle has two wheels.

   _____ + _____

          prefix   root word

2. Joe's teacher let him retake the test.

   _____ + _____

          prefix   root word

3. We visited an underground tunnel on our trip.

   _____ + _____

          prefix   root word

4. If you make a mistake, try to do it again.

   _____ + _____

          prefix   root word

5. You can prevent a fire by remembering not to leave candles lit.

   _____ + _____

          prefix   root word

6. We will uncover the food just before the guests arrive.

   _____ + _____

          prefix   root word

5

© Rosen School Supply•Brain Builders Vocabulary Development•4•RSS-8563-6

Name _____

Synonyms

 Directions: Read the sentences below. Choose a synonym from the box for each underlined word. Write your answers on the lines provided.

permit	argued	observed	goal	rare	give

1. The <u>purpose</u> of the review is to prepare our class for the test.

   _____

2. How much money did she <u>contribute</u> to the charity?

   _____

3. We <u>watched</u> the penguins at the zoo.

   _____

4. Jake and I <u>disagreed</u> about this topic.

   _____

5. Do your parents <u>allow</u> you to stay up this late?

   _____

6. This is a very <u>unusual</u> piece of jewelry.

   _____

© Rosen School Supply•Brain Builders Vocabulary Development•4•RSS-8563-6

Word Classification

 Directions: Circle the word in each group that does not belong.

1. quarter   nickel   penny   wallet

2. shoulder   knee   shirt   wrist

3. grass   tulip   rose   daisy

4. crayon   marker   notebook   pencil

5. juice   pear   milk   water

6. park   museum   theater   bed

7. engineer   brother   doctor   writer

8. ocean   shrimp   crab   lobster

7

Name _____

Homophones

 Directions: Read the sentences below. Choose the best word from the parenthesis to complete each sentence. Write that word on the line.

1. Did you _____ what you want to eat for lunch today? **(chews/choose)**

2. My aunt and uncle named _____ new baby Sam. **(their/there)**

3. I helped my mother build a cabinet out of _____. **(would/wood)**

4. Where did you _____ that beautiful dress? **(bye/buy)**

5. Be careful when you _____ the milk into the glass. **(pour/pore)**

6. Looking directly into the _____ is not good for your eyes. **(sun/son)**

7. My teacher wrote the lesson on the _____. **(bored/board)**

8. Do you _____ if this is the right answer? **(know/no)**

© Rosen School Supply•Brain Builders Vocabulary Development•4•RSS-8563-6

Name _____

K Sounds

 Directions: Choose a word from the box to complete each sentence below. Write that word on the line. Next, circle the letter or letters that make the *k* sound in each word.

| sick | chemistry | stuck | cucumbers | headache | buckle |

1. I will not eat this salad because there are _____ in it.

2. She went to bed early because she had a _____.

3. We will take a _____ class in school next year.

4. Since the _____ on this belt is broken, I will buy a new belt.

5. There is a kitten _____ in that tree.

6. I will stay in bed today because I feel _____.

9

Teaching Tips...

TEACHING TIPS

Background

- An understanding of long and short vowels helps learners identify different language sounds. Developing a sense of these sounds and how they work together to make up words is essential for achieving reading and writing success.

Homework Helper

- After learners have completed the activity on page 14, explain that another way to create a long *a* sound is by using the letters *ay*. Offer learners several examples of this spelling pattern and then have them come up with their own lists of words that follow it.

Research-based Activity

- Introduce learners to the pronunciation keys used in dictionaries. Explain several major sounds, including several long and short vowel sounds. Next, provide learners with a list of words based on those featured in this section's activities. Have them use a dictionary to look up the pronunciation for each word.

Test Prep

- The activities in this section prepare learners for classroom testing on vowel sounds. As this is an important concept for learners to master at this level, extensive practice in this area is necessary.

Different Audiences

- Help a learner for whom English is a second language (ESL) master the difficult concept of vowel sounds by creating flash cards. Write a vowel sound on one side of each card and the different ways to spell that sound, with examples, on the other side. The learner can use these cards as a reference tool while completing activities.

Group Activity

- Divide learners into groups. Assign each group a different long or short vowel sound. Have group members work together to see how many words they can list that feature their assigned vowel sound.

10

Name _____

Short Vowel Sounds

> Vowels can make long and short sounds. Short vowel sounds sound like the *a* in *apple*, the *e* in *egg*, the *i* in *sick*, the *o* in *hop*, and the *u* in *cup*.
> *Examples:* The words *back, end, pit, flop,* and *pup* all have short vowel sounds.

 Directions: Say the name of each picture below. Listen for the short vowel sounds. Write the missing vowel that makes that sound on the line.

1. tr_____ck

2. _____pple

3. b_____lt

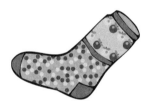

4. s_____ck

5. p_____n

6. cr_____b

 **Think of adjectives that describe the nouns pictured above. Write down the adjectives that have short vowel sounds.**

© Rosen School Supply•Brain Builders Vocabulary Development•4•RSS-8563-6

Name _____

Same Sound

Vowels can make long and short sounds. Short vowel sounds sound like the
a in *hat*, the *e* in *ten*, the *i* in *sit*, the *o* in *top*, and the *u* in *cut*.
Examples: The words *mat*, *pen*, *pin*, *drop*, and *fun* all have short vowel sounds.

 **Directions: Circle the word or words in each group that have
the same short vowel sound as the bold word.**

1. **wind**	tan	fish	tin	ton
2. **vast**	let	trim	swift	has
3. **shut**	lean	sun	cart	nut
4. **test**	mess	roof	day	rest
5. **flop**	art	rob	bet	up
6. **still**	trick	wire	chip	tart
7. **lash**	lick	mask	nap	lake
8. **mob**	knot	mole	pool	nod

 **Make your own list of words with the same short vowel sounds as
the bold words above.**

© Rosen School Supply•Brain Builders Vocabulary Development•4•RSS-8563-6

Long *E* Sound Puzzler

A long vowel sound has the same sound as its name. The long e sound can be spelled *ea* as in *read* or *ee* as in *peer*.

Examples: In the word *wheat*, the long e sound is spelled *ea*.

In the word *street*, the long e sound is spelled *ee*.

 Directions: Fill in the crossword puzzle by choosing a word from the box that matches each clue below.

teach
scream
clean
green
freeze

ACROSS

1. to make very cold

2. to yell loudly

3. opposite of dirty

DOWN

1. a color

2. to instruct

© Rosen School Supply•Brain Builders Vocabulary Development•4•RSS-8563-6

Name _____

The Long A Sound

A long vowel sound has the same sound as its name. The long *a* sound can be spelled *a* as in *acorn*, *ai* as in *pail*, or *a-e* as in *cake*.

Examples: In the word *apron*, the long *a* sound is spelled *a*.

In the word *tail*, the long *a* sound is spelled *ai*.

In the word *rake*, the long *a* sound is spelled *a-e*.

 Directions: Circle all of the words below that have a long *a* sound.

grade	mark	lace	flap
card	wait	claim	barrel
lazy	tape	palm	rage
grain	tackle	grape	plate

 **Make a list of ten words that have a long *a* sound.**

© Rosen School Supply•Brain Builders Vocabulary Development•4•RSS-8563-6

Name _____

Skill Check—Vowel Sounds

Short Vowels

 Directions: Circle the word or words in each group that have the same short vowel sound as the bold word.

1. tap   rat   race   bell

2. send   bind   rest   twin

3. thumb   bug   truck   limb

4. brick   luck   pinch   chill

5. brag   crate   stack   scrap

Long Vowels

 Directions: Circle all the words below that have a long *e* sound.

seat   bring   blend   eagle

bench   feet   leave   desk

© Rosen School Supply•Brain Builders Vocabulary Development•4•RSS-8563-6

Teaching Tips...

Background

- Prefix and suffix recognition helps learners develop strong vocabularies. Since a large portion of the English language is made up of root words paired with prefixes and suffixes, it is important for learners to use their knowledge of word parts to determine the meaning of unknown words.

Homework Helper

- Provide learners with a list of five new prefixes and five new suffixes not found in this section. Have learners write sentences that contain words that involve these prefixes and suffixes.

Research-based Activity

- For a fun and different research activity, have learners use the Internet to find the three longest words in the English language. After learners have found the words, explain the definitions in simple terms. Next, have learners circle the many prefixes and suffixes that make up each word.

Test Prep

- Standardized tests often feature sections testing learners' vocabularies. Since they are not allowed to use a dictionary to answer test questions, learners will draw on their knowledge of prefix and suffix meanings to decode word definitions.

Different Audiences

- Challenge an accelerated learner by having him or her create words with both prefixes and suffixes. Provide the learner with a prefix list, a base word list, and a suffix list. Have the learner mix and match the word parts to see how many words he or she can create.

Group Activity

Separate learners into small groups. Assign each group the same passage to read. Next, have them use a highlighter to identify all of the prefixes and suffixes used in the passage. Once they have finished, have learners discuss the importance of prefixes and suffixes in the English language.

TEACHING TIPS

© Rosen School Supply•Brain Builders Vocabulary Development•4•RSS-8563-6

Name _____

Making New Words

A prefix is a word part added to the beginning of a root word. Adding a prefix changes the meaning of the root word.

Example: In the word *unpaid*, the prefix *un* was added to the root word *paid*. The prefix means *not*, so the new word means *not paid*.

 Directions: Use the prefixes and root words below to make new words. On the lines provided, write five sentences using the words you come up with. Use a separate sheet of paper if you need more space.

Prefixes	
dis	(the opposite of)
re	(again)
un	(not)
pre	(wrong)
mis	(wrong)

Root Words
happy
write
view
obey
understanding

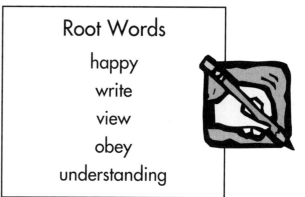

1. _____

2. _____

3. _____

4. _____

5. _____

 **Think of other root words that can be used with these prefixes. Combine these root words with the prefixes to write five new words.**

© Rosen School Supply•Brain Builders Vocabulary Development•4•RSS-8563-6

Name _____

Prefixes

Prefixes and Root Words

A prefix is a word part added to the beginning of a root word. Adding a prefix changes the meaning of the root word.

Example: In the word *nonsense*, the prefix *non* was added to the root word *sense*. The prefix means *no*, so the new word means *no sense*

 Directions: Circle the word in each sentence that begins with a prefix. On the lines, write the prefix and the root word.

1. I could not unzip my jacket because the zipper was stuck.

   _____ + _____
       prefix   root word

2. It will take her a few days to recover from being sick.

   _____ + _____
       prefix   root word

3. That is a very unusual painting.

   _____ + _____
       prefix   root word

4. If you pour any more juice into that glass it will overflow.

   _____ + _____
       prefix   root word

 Write your own sentences using the words you circled above.

18

Name _____

Suffixes and Root Words

A suffix is a word part added to the end of a root word. Adding a suffix changes the meaning of the root word.

Example: In the word *joyful*, the suffix *ful* was added to the word *joy*. The suffix means *full of*, so the new word means *full of joy*.

 Directions: The suffix *less* means *without*. Add this suffix to each root word below. Write the new word on the first line. Next, write the definition of the new word on the second line.

1. humor _____

   _____

2. care _____

   _____

3. tooth _____

   _____

4. flaw _____

   _____

5. use _____

   _____

© Rosen School Supply•Brain Builders Vocabulary Development•4•RSS-8563-6

Name _____

Special Suffixes

A suffix is a word part added to the end of a root word. Adding a suffix changes the meaning of the root word. When we add a suffix to a word that ends in a consonant followed by a *y*, we change the *y* to an *i*.
Example: happy + ness = happiness

 Directions: Combine the root words and suffixes below. Write each new word on the line provided.

1. sorry + est = _____

2. tricky + er = _____

3. marry + ed = _____

4. sticky + est = _____

5. worry + er = _____

6. lucky + est = _____

7. heavy + er = _____

8. occupy + ed = _____

 **Think of another word that ends in a consonant followed by a *y*. Add a suffix to that word, changing the *y* to an *i*.**

© Rosen School Supply•Brain Builders Vocabulary Development•4•RSS-8563-6

Name _____

Skill Check—Prefixes and Suffixes

Prefixes

 Directions: Use the prefixes and root words below to make new words.

Prefixes	Root Words
un	paid
pre	spell
mis	finished

1. _____

2. _____

3. _____

Suffixes

 Directions: The suffix *ful* means *full of*. Write six words using the suffix *ful*.

1. _____   2. _____

3. _____   4. _____

5. _____   6. _____

© Rosen School Supply•Brain Builders Vocabulary Development•4•RSS-8563-6

Teaching Tips...

Background

- Synonyms and antonyms build on learners' prior knowledge of word definitions. As learners complete the activities in this section, they develop a broader vocabulary. This extended vocabulary will encourage learners to write in a more mature and less repetitive style.

Homework Helper

- Introduce learners to antonym pairs that are created by the addition or subtraction of a prefix, such as *happy* and *unhappy*. Have learners see how many pairs they can think of that follow the pattern.

Research-based Activity

- Have learners use a thesaurus to make synonym and antonym lists. By this level, learners should understand how to use a thesaurus. Extra practice in this area will ensure learners are comfortable using this invaluable reference tool.

Test Prep

- Standardized tests frequently feature sections on synonyms and antonyms as a method of measuring vocabulary development. This section will better prepare learners to succeed on these tests.

Different Audiences

- Help a challenged learner understand the difference between synonyms and antonyms by using alliteration. Teach the learner to remember that *synonym* and *same* both start with the letter *s*. This will enable the learner to understand that synonyms have the same meaning.

Group Activity

- Play the memory game with synonyms and antonyms. Groups can make their own tiles or you can make them beforehand. Take the pairs of synonym and antonym tiles and mix them around. Make sure each member of the group has seen all the tiles. Then turn the tiles over. Learners can pick up a tile and try to find the matching synonym or antonym. The person in the group with the most matching pairs wins.

22

Synonyms

Name _____

Matching Meanings

Synonyms are words that have the same or almost the same meaning.
Example: The words *sad* and *unhappy* are synonyms.

 Directions: Choose a synonym from the box to replace the underlined word in each sentence. Write your answers on the lines provided.

| chef | villages | boast | middle | gifts |

1. I received many <u>presents</u> for my birthday. _____

2. We passed through many <u>towns</u> as we drove across

   the state. _____

3. It isn't nice to <u>brag</u> about what you have.

   _____

4. After eating dinner at the restaurant, we went into the kitchen to meet

   the <u>cook</u>. _____

5. We arranged to meet in the <u>center</u> of the park near the fountain.

   _____

© Rosen School Supply•Brain Builders Vocabulary Development•4•RSS-8563-6

Name _____

Color the Cards

Synonyms are words that have the same or almost the same meaning.
Example: The words *mean* and *cruel* are synonyms.

 Directions: There are six pairs of synonyms below. Color each pair with a different color crayon.

| allow | emotion | speak | shy |

| riches | talk | horrify | scare |

| bashful | treasure | permit | feeling |

 **Make your own synonym pairs, mix them up, and trade with a partner or friend.**

© Rosen School Supply•Brain Builders Vocabulary Development•4•RSS-8563-6

Name _____

Opposites

Antonyms are words with opposite meanings.
Example: The words *asleep* and *awake* are antonyms.

 Directions: Draw a line from each word on the left to its antonym on the right.

forget	reward

punish	follow

question	expensive

lead	remember

cheap	answer

Write three more pairs of antonyms on your own.

© Rosen School Supply•Brain Builders Vocabulary Development•4•RSS-8563-6

Name _____

Find the Antonym

Antonyms are words with opposite meanings.
Example: The words *beginning* and *end* are antonyms.

 Directions: Find an antonym for the underlined word in each sentence below. Write your answers on the lines provided.

| dull | bitter | lend | friends | rude | empty |

1. May I please <u>borrow</u> this book? _____

2. It is <u>polite</u> to say "thank you" after someone gives you something.

   _____

3. You must be careful when you are using a <u>sharp</u> knife.

   _____

4. Do not speak to <u>strangers</u> on the street. _____

5. Fruit tastes good because it is <u>sweet</u>. _____

6. My glass is <u>full</u>. _____

 **Think of a synonym for each underlined word.**

© Rosen School Supply•Brain Builders Vocabulary Development•4•RSS-8563-6

Name _____

Skill Check—Synonyms and Antonyms

Synonyms

 Directions: Match each word on the left to its synonym on the right.

courage	love
adore	top
cover	bravery

Antonyms

 Directions: Match each word on the left to its antonym on the right.

noisy	never
always	above
below	silent

27

© Rosen School Supply•Brain Builders Vocabulary Development•4•RSS-8563-6

Teaching Tips...

Background
- In this section, learners develop their abilities to compare, contrast, and analyze words. In classifying words and completing analogies, learners build their vocabularies and critical reasoning skills.

Homework Helper
- Have learners practice creating analogies using those featured in the activity on page 31. Ask learners to look at the first pair of words in each question and think of a second pair that fits the first pair's relationship.

Research-based Activity
- After completing the activity on page 29, have learners do further research about the Revolutionary War. Have each learner choose a topic of interest, such as a specific battle, and write a report about what they discover.

Test Prep
- Analogies are frequently featured on standardized tests, at this level and in higher grades, in order to test learners' critical thinking skills. The activities in this section provide practice for learners in this area.

Different Audiences
- Help a challenged learner grasp the concept of analogies. Explain how to look for the relationship between words by rearranging the words or writing a sentence about them. For example, using the analogy "Sand is to grains as water is to ?," a learner might explain the relationship between grain and sand as sand being made up of grains. After grasping this relationship, the learner can determine what water is made up of and complete the analogy with the word *drops*.

Group Activity
- Divide learners into groups. Have each group work together to classify various objects in the classroom. Once they have finished, groups can compare classifications. This exercise allows learners to gain insight from their peers.

28

Word Classification

Name _____

The Revolutionary War

Classification is putting similar things into a group.
Example: We can classify a dog, a cat, and a rabbit as pets.

 Directions: Read the paragraph below. Make four lists that classify different things mentioned in the paragraph. Use a separate sheet of paper if you need more space.

The American Revolutionary War, which started in 1775, was fought between Great Britain and the thirteen American colonies. Many battles were fought in what would become the states of Massachusetts, Pennsylvania, and New York. George Washington was the leader of the American army. William Howe was in charge of the British army. The war ended in 1783 when a treaty was signed recognizing the United States of America as an independent nation.

<u>States</u>   <u>Countries</u>

_____   _____

_____   _____

_____

<u>People</u>   <u>Years</u>

_____   _____

_____   _____

 **Look around your bedroom. Find three different groups of things you can classify.**

© Rosen School Supply•Brain Builders Vocabulary Development•4•RSS-8563-6

Name _____

Word Groups

Classification is putting similar things into a group.
Example: We can classify apples, oranges, and bananas as fruits.

 Directions: Circle the word in each group that does not belong.

1. tic-tac-toe   planting   chess   hopscotch

2. juice   fruit   lemonade   milk

3. nail   hammer   wrench   pliers

4. football   soccer   computer   golf

5. grapes   broccoli   carrots   celery

6. paint   draw   color   erase

7. scarf   gloves   T-shirt   overcoat

8. aunt   father   friend   grandfather

 **Think of another word that can be classified in each group above.**

30

© Rosen School Supply•Brain Builders Vocabulary Development•4•RSS-8563-6

Name _____

How Do the Words Go Together?

An analogy is a relationship between two pairs of words. We figure out how the first pair of words goes together in order to complete the second pair. *Example: Cat* is to *meow* as *dog* is to ___?___. The relationship between the first pair of words is animal to sound. A cat meows and a dog barks. The answer is *bark*.

 Directions: Read the analogies below. Use the relationship between the first pair of words in each one to complete the second pair. Write your answers on the lines. The first one has been done for you.

1. Hat is to head as scarf is to **neck** _____.

2. Drive is to car as fly is to _____.

3. Up is to down as day is to _____.

4. Sight is to eyes as smell is to _____.

5. Toe is to foot as finger is to _____.

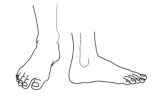

 **Think of your own analogy.**

© Rosen School Supply•Brain Builders Vocabulary Development•4•RSS-8563-6

Name _____

Analogy Puzzler

An analogy is a relationship between two pairs of words. We figure out how the first pair of words go together in order to complete the second pair. *Example: Up* is to *down* as *fast* is to ___?___. The relationship between the first pair of words is that they are opposites. *Up* is the opposite of *down* and *fast* is the opposite of *slow*. The answer is *slow*.

👉 **Directions: Complete the analogy clues to fill in the crossword puzzle.**

Across

1. Day is to week as month is to _____.

2. Apple is to fruit as steak is to _____.

3. Neck is to necklace as finger is to _____

4. Cow is to farm as dolphin is to _____.

Down

1. Woman is to man as female is to _____.

2. Page is to book as branch is to _____.

© Rosen School Supply•Brain Builders Vocabulary Development•4•RSS-8563-6

Name _____

Skill Check—Word Classification and Analogies

Word Classification

 Directions: Circle the word in each group that does not belong.

1. angry   happy   encourage   sad

2. lake   stream   ocean   dam

3. story   cartoon   play   poem

3. morning   evening   week   afternoon

Analogies

 Directions: Complete each analogy below.

1. Inch is to foot as ounce is to _____.

2. Sun is to day as moon is to _____.

3. Girl is to daughter as boy is to _____.

© Rosen School Supply•Brain Builders Vocabulary Development•4•RSS-8563-6

Teaching Tips...

For *Homophones and Syllables* (pp. 35–39)

Background

- In this section, learners work with homophones and practice determining the number of syllables in a word. Learners gain a deeper understanding of spelling by recognizing that words that sound the same are often entirely different. Working with syllables strengthens learners' abilities to read unfamiliar words, enabling them to become independent readers.

Homework Helper

- Have learners create their own lists of homophones. Learners can involve their family members to see how many homophones they can think of together.

Research-based Activity

- Have learners use the Internet or their local libraries to find out more information about polar bear cubs. Ask learners to write a report about what they have learned, including pictures.

Test Prep

- The activities in this section help prepare learners for standardized testing at the fourth-grade level. Homophones and syllables are concepts that learners should be familiar with at this age.

Different Audiences

- Encourage a learner for whom English is a second language (ESL) to keep a homophone journal. Have the learner write down any homophones that he or she encounters in his or her reading, both inside and outside of the classroom. Have the learner use a dictionary to find definitions for the words. This exercise will help the learner memorize unfamiliar words.

Group Activity

- Divide learners into groups. Assign each group a different song and show them how to clap out the rhythm for each one. Next, have each group discuss how clapping out various beats is related to syllables.

© Rosen School Supply•Brain Builders Vocabulary Development•4•RSS-8563-6

Name _____

Polar Bear Cubs

Homophones are words that sound the same but are spelled differently and have different meanings.

Example: The words *write* and *right* are homophones. While they sound the same, *write* is something you do with a pencil and *right* means correct.

 Directions: Read the sentences below. Choose the correct word from the parenthesis to complete each sentence. Write the word on the line.

1. Polar bear cubs are born with their eyes closed. They have no sense of _____ for the first few weeks of their lives.   (**sight/site**)

2. Polar bear cubs begin to walk at around _____ months of age.

   (**too/two**)

3. As polar bear cubs grow older _____ paws become very big.

   (**their/there**)

4. By the time they are eight months old, polar bear cubs can _____ close to 100 pounds (45 kilograms).   (**way/weigh**)

5. Polar bear cubs learn to hunt _____, such as seals, walruses, fish, and whales.   (**pray/prey**)

 Use a dictionary to find a definition for each homophone you didn't use.

35

© Rosen School Supply•Brain Builders Vocabulary Development•4•RSS-8563-6

Homophones

Words That Sound the Same

Homophones are words that sound the same but are spelled differently and have different meanings.

Example: The words *sore* and *soar* are homophones. While they sound the same, *sore* describes a painful feeling and *soar* is to fly very high.

 Directions: Read the sentences below. Choose the best word from the parenthesis to complete each sentence. Write that word on the line.

1. I saw an _____ in the newspaper for a product I want to buy.

   (add/ad)

2. Mom was ready to leave for school, but I had _____ brushed my teeth.   (knot/not)

3. The song had a familiar drum _____.   (beat/beet)

4. On our camping trip, we set our tent up near a _____.

   (creak/creek)

5. The ship docked at the _____.   (pier/peer)

6. I have looked everywhere and I cannot _____ that book.   (fined/find)

 **Write your own sentences using each of the unused homophones above.**

36

Name _____

Syllable Lists

Words are made up of parts called syllables. A syllable is a part of a word that has its own sound. Every syllable has a vowel sound.
Example: The word *carnival* has 3 syllables.   car • ni • val

 Directions: Look at the words in the box. Write the one-syllable words in the one-syllable list, the two-syllable words in the two-syllable list, the three-syllable words in the three-syllable list, and the four-syllable words in the four-syllable list.

| contrast | pearl | marvelous | generation |
| widow | telephone | ingredient | fuse |

ONE-SYLLABLE WORDS

_____

_____

TWO-SYLLABLE WORDS

_____

_____

THREE-SYLLABLE WORDS

_____

_____

FOUR-SYLLABLE WORDS

_____

_____

 Think of your own words to add to each group.

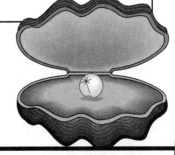

© Rosen School Supply•Brain Builders Vocabulary Development•4•RSS-8563-6

Name _____

Same Syllables

Words are made up of parts called syllables. A syllable is a part of a word that has its own sound. Every syllable has a vowel sound.

Example: The word *paradise* has three syllables.   par • a • dise

 Directions: Read the words in each group. Circle the word or words that have the same number of syllables as the word in bold.

1. **ballet**   graduate   error   outcome

2. **lump**   forest   carve   echo

3. **wilderness**   tablecloth   storm   happiness

4. **discontinue**   interfere   scramble   economy

5. **assemble**   fingernail   encounter   particular

6. **rescue**   slug   review   potato

7. **continent**   concrete   detective   tired

8. **relate**   remark   proportion   tumble

 **Figure out how many syllables there are in your name.**

© Rosen School Supply•Brain Builders Vocabulary Development•4•RSS-8563-6

Name _____

Skill Check—Homophones and Syllables

Homophones

Directions: Read the sentences below. Choose the correct homophone from the parenthesis to complete each sentence.

1. Shoshanna broke her _____ and could not walk to school.
   (toe/tow)

2. I wear a belt around my _____. (waste/waist)

3. We could not finish the _____ pizza by ourselves. (hole/whole)

Syllables

Directions: Read the words below. Write the number of syllables in each word on the line.

1. forever _____   5. cabbage _____

2. mainly _____   6. humble _____

3. impossible _____ 7. gown _____

4. accident _____   8. lazy _____

© Rosen School Supply•Brain Builders Vocabulary Development•4•RSS-8563-6

Teaching Tips...

Background

- This section focuses on how different letters can form *k*, *s*, and *f* sounds. It is important for learners at this level to gain an appreciation and understanding of letters making various sounds. Learners can employ this skill to sound out unfamiliar words they encounter while reading.

Homework Helper

- Have learners write lists of words with *k* sounds. Have each learner make a list of words that use the letter *k*, the letter *c*, the letters *ch*, and the letters *ck* to make *k* sounds. Once finished, learners can compare their lists to broaden their vocabularies.

Research-based Activity

- After they have completed the activity on page 41, have learners use the Internet to research the components that make up a balanced diet. Next, have learners write a report detailing their findings. For extra fun, have learners find a healthy recipe to bring in as well.

Test Prep

- The activities in this section help prepare learners for both classroom and standardized testing. By learning various ways of spelling sounds, learners develop their abilities to recognize unfamiliar words in texts.

Different Audiences

- Challenge an accelerated learner by introducing him or her to other spelling sounds. For example, you might introduce the long *u* sound, spelled *u-e*, *ew*, *oo*, *o-e*, and *ue*. You might also introduce the learner to the long *i* sound, spelled *i*, *i-e*, and *y*.

Group Activity

- Separate learners into groups. Allow each group to choose a spelling sound, *k*, *s*, or *f*. Next ask each group to write a list of at least 10 words using their letter sound. Finally, have groups create word searches using their list of words. When every group has finished, have them exchange and complete each others' word searches.

TEACHING TIPS

40

Name _____

Sounds Like K

The letter *k* is not the only letter that can make a *k* sound. The letter *c* makes a *k* sound when it is followed by an *a*, an *o*, or a *u*. Together, the letters *ck* or *ch* can also make a *k* sound.

Examples: In the word *career*, the letter *c* makes a *k* sound.

In the word *chorus*, the letters *ch* make a *k* sound.

In the word *back*, the letters *ck* make a *k* sound.

Directions: Choose a word from the box to complete each sentence below. Write that word on the line. Next, circle the letter or letters that make the *k* sound in that word.

broccoli	pick	stomach
combined		chicken

1. A balance of fat, protein, and carbohydrates should be _____ to make up a healthy diet.

2. Protein can be found in meats, such as _____.

3. Try to _____ healthy fruits and vegetables as snacks instead of sweets.

4. _____ is a vegetable with many vitamins your body needs.

5. It is important to fill your _____ with healthy foods.

Think of three healthy foods that have *k* sounds in their names.

41

Name _____

Circle the Letters

The letter *k* is not the only letter that can make a *k* sound. The letter *c* makes a *k* sound when it is followed by an *a*, an *o*, or a *u*. Together, the letters *ck* or *ch* can also make a *k* sound.

Examples: In the word *cook*, the letter *k* makes the *k* sound.

In the word *crane*, the letter *c* makes the *k* sound.

In the word *orchid*, the letters *ch* make the *k* sound.

In the word *wick*, the letters *ck* make the *k* sound.

 Directions: Circle the letter or letters that make a *k* sound in each word below.

1. tackle

2. chameleon

3. blank

4. check

5. stuck

6. practical

 **Write down your own list of words that use *k*, *c*, *ch*, and *ck* to make the *k* sound.**

© Rosen School Supply•Brain Builders Vocabulary Development•4•RSS-8563-6

Name _____

What Makes the *S* Sound?

The letter *s* is not the only letter that can make an *s* sound. The letter *c* makes an *s* sound when it is followed by the letters *e, i,* or *y*. Together, the letters *sc* can also make the *s* sound.

Examples: In the word *sell*, the letter *s* makes the *s* sound.

In the word *celery*, the letter *c* makes the *s* sound.

In the word *scissors*, the letters *sc* make the *s* sound.

 Directions: Choose a word from the box to complete each sentence below. Next, circle the letter or letters in that word that make the *s* sound.

decide	syrup	house	science	citizen	scenery

1. My class is helping paint the _____ for the school play.

2. Our neighbors are moving to a new _____.

3. I cannot _____ what I want to eat for dinner.

4. We learned about the parts of a plant in _____ class today.

5. If you are a _____ of the United States, you have certain rights.

6. I like to pour maple _____ over my pancakes.

© Rosen School Supply•Brain Builders Vocabulary Development•4•RSS-8563-6

Name _____

Fun with the Letter *F*

The letter *f* is not the only letter that can make an *f* sound. Together, the letters *ph* can make an *f* sound. Together, the letters *gh* can also make an *f* sound. *Examples:* In the word *famous*, the letter *f* makes an *f* sound.

In the word *phone*, the letters *ph* make an *f* sound.

In the word *laugh*, the letters *gh* make an *f* sound.

 Directions: Circle the letter or letters that make an *f* sound in each word below.

1. elephant

2. few

3. cough

4. forest

5. photo

6. phrase

7. enough

8. alphabet

9. female

 **Think of another word that uses either *ph* or *gh* to make an *f* sound.**

© Rosen School Supply•Brain Builders Vocabulary Development•4•RSS-8563-6

Name _____

Skill Check—Spelling Sounds

K Sounds

 Directions: First, use a green marker to circle the words below that use the letter *k* to make a *k* sound. Next, use a blue marker to circle the words that use the letters *ck* to make a *k* sound. Finally, use a yellow marker to circle all of the words that use the letters *ch* to make a *k* sound.

package	back
talk	sick
spike	wicked
anchor	kind

S Sounds

 Directions: Circle the letter or letters in each word that make an *s* sound.

1. piece   2. similar

3. vast   4. scissors

5. cement   6. cell

© Rosen School Supply•Brain Builders Vocabulary Development•4•RSS-8563-6

Answer Key

p. 4

1. *smell* and *beg* should be circled

2. *grasp* should be circled

3. *fetch* and *bench* should be circled

4. *fist* and *thick* should be circled

5. *stuck* and *shrug* should be circled

6. *doll* and *clock* should be circled

7. *blast* and *raft* should be circled

8. *duck* and *bun* should be circled

p. 5

1. *bicycle* should be circled; bi + cycle

2. *retake* should be circled; re + take

3. *underground* should be circled; under + ground

4. *mistake* should be circled; mis + take

5. *prevent* should be circled; pre + vent

6. *uncover* should be circled; un + cover

p. 6

1. goal
2. give
3. observed
4. argued
5. permit
6. rare

p. 7

1. *wallet* should be circled

2. *shirt* should be circled

3. *grass* should be circled

4. *notebook* should be circled

5. *pear* should be circled

6. *bed* should be circled

7. *brother* should be circled

8. *ocean* should be circled

p. 8

1. choose
2. their
3. wood
4. buy
5. pour
6. sun
7. board
8. know

p. 9

1. cucumbers; *c* should be circled twice

2. headache; *ch* should be circled

3. chemistry; *ch* should be circled

4. buckle; *ck* should be circled

5. stuck; *ck* should be circled

6. sick; *ck* should be circled

p. 11

1. u
2. a
3. e
4. o
5. i
6. a

p. 12

1. *fish* and *tin* should be circled

2. *has* should be circled

3. *sun* and *nut* should be circled

4. *mess* and *rest* should be circled

5. *rob* should be circled

6. *trick* and *chip* should be circled

7. *mask* and *nap* should be circled

8. *knot* and *nod* should be circled

p. 13

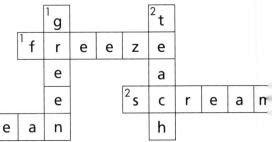

p. 14

grade, lace, wait, claim, lazy, tape, rage, grain, grape, and *plate* should be circled

p. 15

Short Vowels

1. *rat* should be circled

2. *rest* should be circled

3. *bug* and *truck* should be circled

4. *pinch* and *chill* should be circled

5. *stack* and *scrap* should be circled

© Rosen School Supply•Brain Builders Vocabulary Development•4•RSS-8563-6

Long Vowels

seat, *eagle*, *feet*, and *leave* should be circled

p. 17
Answers will vary.

p. 18
1. *unzip* should be circled; un + zip
2. *recover* should be circled; re + cover
3. *unusual* should be circled; un + usual
4. *overflow* should be circled; over + flow

p. 19
1. humorless; without humor
2. careless; without care
3. toothless; without teeth
4. flawless; without flaws
5. useless; without use

p. 20
1. sorriest
2. trickier
3. married
4. stickiest
5. worrier
6. luckiest
7. heavier
8. occupied

p. 21
Prefixes
Answers will vary.

Suffixes
Answers will vary.

p. 23
1. gifts
2. villages
3. boast
4. chef
5. middle

p. 24
Synonym pairs: allow/permit, emotion/feeling, speak/talk, shy/bashful, riches/treasure, horrify/scare

p. 25

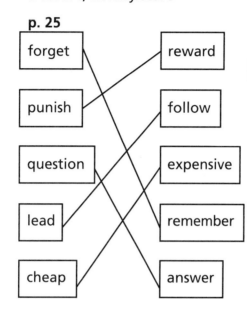

p. 26
1. lend
2. rude
3. dull
4. friends
5. bitter
6. empty

p. 27
Synonyms

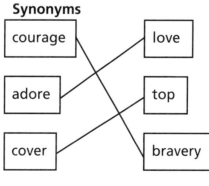

Antonyms

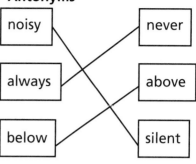

p. 29
States: Massachusetts, Pennsylvania, New York
Countries: Great Britain, United States of America
People: George Washington, William Howe
Years: 1775, 1783

p. 30
1. *planting* should be circled
2. *fruit* should be circled
3. *nail* should be circled
4. *computer* should be circled
5. *grapes* should be circled
6. *erase* should be circled
7. *T-shirt* should be circled
8. *friend* should be circled

p. 31
1. neck
2. plane
3. night
4. nose
5. hand

p. 32

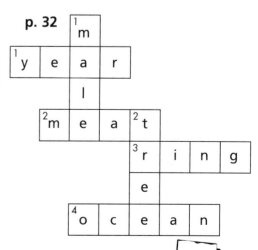

47

p. 33
Word Classification
1. *encourage* should be circled
2. *dam* should be circled
3. *cartoon* should be circled
4. *week* should be circled

Analogies
1. pound
2. night
3. son

p. 35
1. sight
2. two
3. their
4. weigh
5. prey

p. 36
1. ad
2. not
3. beat
4. creek
5. pier
6. find

p. 37
1. one-syllable words: pearl, fuse
2. two-syllable words: contrast, widow
3. three-syllable words: marvelous, telephone
4. four-syllable words: generation, ingredient

p. 38
1. *error* and *outcome* should be circled
2. *carve* should be circled
3. *tablecloth* and *happiness* should be circled
4. *economy* should be circled

5. *fingernail* and *encounter* should be circled
6. *review* should be circled
7. *detective* should be circled
8. *remark* and *tumble* should be circled

p. 39
Homophones
1. toe
2. waist
3. whole

Syllables
1. 3
2. 2
3. 4
4. 3
5. 2
6. 2
7. 1
8. 2

p. 41
1. combined; *c* should be circled
2. chicken; *ck* should be circled
3. pick; *ck* should be circled
4. Broccoli; *cc* should be circled
5. stomach; *ch* should be circled

p. 42
1. *ck* should be circled
2. *ch* should be circled
3. *k* should be circled
4. *ck* should be circled
5. *ck* should be circled
6. *c* should be circled

p. 43
1. scenery; *sc* should be circled
2. house; *s* should be circled
3. decide; *c* should be circled
4. science; *sc* should be circled
5. syrup; *s* should be circled

p. 44
1. *ph* should be circled
2. *f* should be circled
3. *gh* should be circled
4. *f* should be circled
5. *ph* should be circled
6. *ph* should be circled
7. *gh* should be circled
8. *ph* should be circled
9. *f* should be circled

p. 45
K Sounds
talk, *spike*, and *kind* should be circled in green

package, *sick*, *back*, and *wicked* should be circled in blue

anchor should be circled in yellow

S Sounds
1. *ce* should be circled
2. *s* should be circled
3. *s* should be circled
4. *sc* should be circled
5. *c* should be circled
6. *c* should be circled.

© Rosen School Supply•Brain Builders Vocabulary Development•4•RSS-8563-6